THE GOLDEN AGE OF JAZZ

On-location portraits, in words and pictures, of more than 200 outstanding musicians from the late '30s through the '40s

TEXT AND PHOTOGRAPHS BY

William P. Gottlieb

SIMON AND SCHUSTER ■ NEW YORK

The author is grateful for the editorial assistance of Walter Schaap and Roslyn Snow.

The photographs in this book were taken between 1939 and 1948. They were made with a Speed Graphic, a Graflex, and a Rolleiflex; the principal source of artificial light was flashbulbs. The prints come from the Edward J. Gottlieb Collection. Enlargements from the original negatives are available through Photo-Graphics, Inc., P.O. Box 57248, West End Station, Washington, D.C. 20007.

Published by Simon and Schuster
A Division of Gulf & Western Corporation
Simon & Schuster Building
Rockefeller Center
1230 Avenue of the Americas
New York, New York 10020

Designed by Libra Graphics, Inc.
Manufactured in the United States of America

1   2   3   4   5   6   7   8   9   10

Library of Congress Cataloging in Publication Data

Gottlieb, William P
    The golden age of jazz.

    Includes index.
    1.   Jazz musicians—Portraits.   2.   Jazz music—
Pictorial works.   I.   Title.
ML3561.J3G63   779'.2   78–31288

ISBN   0–671–24375–6
          0–671–24730–1 Pbk.

This book is dedicated to Walter Schaap
and to his son Philip, who, each in his own way,
have done so much to strengthen the beat of jazz.

CONTENTS

Louis Armstrong

INTRODUCTION

by JOHN S. WILSON

Jazz Critic, *The New York Times*

For most of us, the Golden Age of Jazz turns out to be the time when we first discovered the music—when we were hit or, more likely, overwhelmed by a shock of joyous recognition. In retrospect, nothing can ever equal the genius of the musicians who were playing then, when we first found the music, although we may admit to the unusual abilities of certain giants of an earlier age or, more grudgingly, of an occasional innovator who came afterward.

For Bill Gottlieb—and for me—the Golden Age of Jazz occurred in the late '30s and the '40s. It had to be a Golden Age when one could experience the constant sense of discovery that was possible then. It was a time when such then veterans as Jelly Roll Morton, Sidney Bechet, James P. Johnson, Fats Waller, and Willie "The Lion" Smith—masters of the music in the '20s—were re-emerging. It was a time when that unique institution, the big band, was at its peak: Jimmie Lunceford's magnificent mixture of show biz and hip jazz; Earl Hines' gloriously swinging Grand Terrace band; Count Basie honing a marvelous musical instrument out of the elements of a Kansas City jam session; Duke Ellington moving the greatest of all the big bands, his 1940–41 group, into the swampy, uncharted waters of extended composition.

It was a time when the past was being constantly restated—the so-called "Chicago jazz" of the late '20s by Pee Wee Russell, Bud Freeman, Wild Bill Davison, and other veterans of those Chicago days who became part of the Eddie Condon repertory company in New York; the earlier Chicago jazz direct from New Orleans, played by King Oliver and Louis Armstrong, which inspired Lu Watters and Bob Scobey and Turk Murphy in San Francisco; and the more direct line to old New Orleans provided by Bunk Johnson and George Lewis. And it was a time when so many new ideas came tumbling out on the jazz scene that they finally coalesced in a musical revolution—in bebop: Lester Young, followed by Charlie Christian and Jimmy Blanton, who were followed by Dizzy Gillespie and Charlie Parker and Bud Powell and by Thelonious Monk and Miles Davis.

It was, to say the least, a dazzling period. Every time you turned around, particularly in New York, there was something new on 52nd Street or in Greenwich Village: the hectic three-piano boogie-woogie playing of Meade Lux Lewis, Albert Ammons, and Pete Johnson mixed with Joe Turner's blue shouting at Café Society; Billie Holiday glowing under the huge white gardenia in her hair; the subtle sound of John Kirby's sextet; the powerhouse bands of Woody Herman and Stan Kenton; the "weird" concatenations of the emergent beboppers at the Royal Roost, at Bop City, and, eventually, at Birdland.

Bill Gottlieb landed in the midst of all this—intentionally, and with a fan's enthusiasm, as a writer; unintentionally (as he explains) as a photographer. The combination of the two talents put him in an unusual position. There were others around then who were writing on jazz (I was one of them). And there were others who were taking pictures. But no one else was taking pictures and getting the stories at the same time—a combination that gave Gottlieb's approach to his photography a distinctive, storytelling touch.

In this collection, there are innumerable examples of Gottlieb's inimitable personal touch—his view of the stunned admirer of June Christy; Dizzy Gillespie clowning through Ella Fitzgerald's performance under the questioning eye of her then husband, Ray Brown; the Ellington dressing room; the unusual views of Buddy De Franco intently picking something out on a piano and Sarah Vaughan relaxed in a card game; the remarkable pictorial projection of the vast and voluminous sound of Sidney Bechet on soprano saxophone.

Gottlieb was not there just shooting at random. He was always there with a purpose: there were articles to be written for *The Washington Post*, for *Down Beat, for Collier's*, and he saw his subjects in the contexts of those stories. The pictures that resulted are considered by many connoisseurs to be the best overall photographic reportage of this volatile period of jazz. And in this book, they are supplemented by Gottlieb's recollections of the people he was photographing.

It is a combination that brings these wonderfully vital, creative personalities back into living perspective, a combination of setting and sight that needs only the sound to make it complete. So, as you look at these pictures, get out those old records (many of them are available in reissues) and relive this Golden Age of Jazz. Or, if you missed it—by the accident of birth or because you were not paying proper attention while it was happening—discover it, just the way Bill Gottlieb and I and thousands of others kept discovering it time and time again while it was going on.

JOHN S. WILSON

FOREWORD

The Golden Age of Jazz? It must surely be those jumping years from the late 1930s through the '40s. Despite the Great Depression and World War II, this was a period of enormous musical achievement. During the first half of the era, big-band jazz—mostly under the name *swing*—reached its peak. During the second half, bop and other modern jazz forms developed. And during both halves, audiences had ready access to older styles, much of it played by legendary musicians who had started blowing way back when jazz first began.

The Golden Age had other distinctions: It was the first time that white audiences, in large numbers, began to recognize and appreciate hot music. And it has proved to be the only time when popularity and quality have coincided; when, for once, the most widely acclaimed music was the best music.

I stumbled onto jazz in 1936 while writing a monthly record page for the Lehigh University *Review*. I then went to work for *The Washington Post*, producing, among other things, a weekly music column—one of the first regular newspaper features devoted primarily to jazz. Simultaneously I performed as a disc-jockey on Washington's NBC outlet, WRC, and on an independent station, WINX.

Came the war and the army. While I was in service, my contact with jazz diminished but didn't end; many military bases had swingin' combos. And would you believe that at Yale University, where I received my cadet training, the Glenn Miller orchestra, led by Ray McKinley, played in the mess hall!

After the war I became a writer for the music magazine *Down Beat*. During the next few years I wrote about jazz not only for the *Beat* but for the *Record Changer*, the *Saturday Review*, and *Collier's*. Then in the late '40s I left music for other fields.

From *Washington Post* days I learned that I couldn't expect to get staff photographers to cover my music stories; it would have meant their working on their own time, late at night. To get me off their backs, *Post* photographers taught me to take my own pictures. That's what I've been doing ever since.

In this book it is the pictures that really count; the text is secondary and brief, though each chapter includes one or two extended vignettes of individuals whose personalities especially captivated me.

I interviewed and photographed almost all the outstanding instrumentalists and singers of the time. Pictures of more than 200 of them appear in these pages. An equal number must, for now, remain in my negative files.

Only a handful of the top musicians are missing. In some instances, their paths and mine never crossed. In a few cases, I let a big one get away: Jelly Roll Morton, for example. In 1939 I spent a considerable amount of time with this important pioneer of jazz. He was far past his prime and was holed up in a pathetic little upstairs club on U Street in Washington. Jelly would play for me and for occasional customers, continually interrupting himself with brave talk of how he'd one day get to New York City and reestablish himself as King. I never thought he'd get as far as Baltimore.

But damned if he didn't go to New York and make an historic batch of records for Bluebird/Victor. Though the sessions didn't restore his fortunes, they reminded jazz fans throughout the world that Jelly Roll Morton was indeed one of the great ones. Why didn't I take his picture any of the times I was with him? There was a problem: I hadn't yet learned to use a camera.

Then there's Fats Waller. He was flying from Detroit to play a Washington theater. By phone I made plans to have him appear with me on a radio show. He promised he'd join me soon after his plane landed. The time slot was fixed. The broadcast was publicized. Everything was set. Except Fats. Fats dreaded flying. To drown his fears, he guzzled Old Grand-Dad from takeoff to touchdown, arriving in no condition to face a microphone.

His factotum, saxophonist Gene Sedric, took Fats' place. The show turned out satisfactorily, but I foolishly was piqued and canceled my planned newspaper piece on Fats. That's another photo never taken! Two years later, before I had a second chance, Fats died. (Ironically, on a train!)

So, here is the Golden Age of Jazz without Fats and without Jelly Roll. But almost all of the other hot-music stars are here. They're presented in a way that should help you recall (or first learn about) a remarkable group of artists from a unique period in American music.

THE GOLDEN
AGE
OF JAZZ

1. THAT OLD-TIME JAZZ

During the '30s and '40s there were still plenty of working musicians who had been around when jazz was beginning. They were authentic pioneers but not as old as sometimes depicted. Since most of them were born in the 1890s, the average "old-timer" was still under fifty.

These veterans were a colorful breed, often with extravagant personalities that added pizzazz to their jazz. Musically, however, they were conservative, usually clinging to traditional styles as if the styles were security blankets—which in a way they were, for this was the music the fans expected of them; old-timers departed from it at their peril.

Although old-time jazz had limited appeal during the Golden Age, it did enjoy a substantial renaissance, thanks partly to the general enthusiasm for hot music generated among audiences by the popular swing bands of the era.

The playing of traditional jazz was not entirely confined to the old-timers. The music attracted a number of disciples, some of them only in their teens and all of them fanatical. They were the play-it-like-it-was musicians who, along with equally fervid listeners, found in the old-time jazz just the chord that suited them.

Willie "The Lion" Smith

Old-timer Willie "The Lion" Smith never became one of the paramount kings of jazz, but he couldn't have handled himself in a more regal manner; he dressed splendidly, walked with majestic dignity, held court grandly with his fans, and—with royal self-esteem—habitually referred to himself in the third person. "The Lion is here," he would announce on entering a room. While playing, The Lion sat on the piano stool as if it were a throne. And if the music was going well, he'd swivel sideways on the stool, the better to address his loyal subjects, and issue a series of lordly observations like: "The Lion is laying it down real good tonight!"

The Lion's full name was William Henry Joseph Bonaparte Bertholoff Smith. With all that to choose from, how did he end up calling himself The Lion? The first time I asked, he said he was given his nickname by another legendary pianist, James P. Johnson, in recognition of The Lion's domineering attitude. (In return, The Lion called James P. "The Brute," not because of Johnson's personality, which was pleasant, but because of his imposing body topped by an oversized head.)

About a year after giving me that account of his name, The Lion came up with an entirely different version:

"In the First World War, I was a gunner in a Negro brigade. When our colonel wanted some of us to man a French seventy-five, I volunteered and was up front firing for forty-five days, without relief. The colonel promoted me to sergeant and told everyone I was a 'lion' with a gun. The name stuck."

The Lion once gave a similar account to Timmie Rosenkrantz, a Danish baron turned jazznik. The Lion ended his story with this beautiful coda: "It was a tough war, Timmie, and I'm proud and happy I won it."

Still another time, The Lion gave me a *third* version of how he got his name. "I'm Jewish. I was bar-mitzvahed, speak Yiddish fluently

. . . the whole megilla. I tried to become a rabbi, but because of prejudice the best I could do was study to be a cantor. A cantor's job is mostly music. Naturally, I was great—so great that the rest of the class called me the Lion of Judea."

The Lion then showed me his calling card. On one side was his name, Willie "The Lion" Smith, with his address, phone number, and the title "The Hebrew Cantor," all printed in English. On the other side of the card was the equivalent information in Hebrew.

The Lion's outrageous flamboyance never obscured his talent as a musician. On jump tunes, his rock-solid stride piano could be the driving force behind a band. Yet he could immediately follow with a delicate solo, perhaps his own charming composition "Echoes of Spring."

The Lion was particularly known for his strong left hand. Appropriately, he had a ready roar for piano players who couldn't make full use of all ten fingers. "What's the matter, man —your left hand crippled? Here, let me show you how to do it."

And he did show plenty of piano players "how to do it." Dozens of first-rate jazz pianists acknowledge their debt to him. One of his "students," Duke Ellington, paid tribute by composing and recording "Portrait of The Lion."

Yet it's The Lion's grandiose personality, more than his superb musicianship, that I now most often recall. There's the time the two of us, in Washington, drove by taxi to the Howard Theater, where he was performing. When we arrived and got out of the cab, the driver asked for the fare. Before responding, The Lion slowly and deliberately shepherded me through the stage door, then turned and imperiously announced, "The Lion *never* pays for taxis!"

The driver was too flabbergasted to react. Unchallenged, The Lion joined me inside, after closing the stage door firmly.

James P., "The Brute"

*James P., with Freddie
Moore at drums, Fess
Williams with clarinet, and
trumpeter Joe Thomas,
seated at right.*

James P. Johnson

James P. Johnson didn't have the hubris of
his crony, The Lion, but he was nonetheless
an imposing and important person, probably
the most influential jazz piano player performing between the reigns of Scott Joplin
and Earl Hines. His disciples, including Fats
Waller, dominated a generation of keyboard
artists. Jimmy was also a composer. He wrote
jazz pieces, a symphony, and one of the top
pop hits of the '20s, "Charleston."

By the time I got to know James P., he had
suffered a paralyzing stroke. Although largely
recovered, he had become relatively subdued,
according to friends who recalled his vibrant
days. But, subdued or not, he continued to be
regarded as one of jazz's venerable masters.

When I left the music business to enter the
audio-visual field, it was James P. Johnson
who, with a combo that included Freddy
Moore, Fess Williams, and Joe Thomas, played
at my office opening—which is where I took
one of the pictures on this page.

Huddie "Leadbelly" Ledbetter

Leadbelly, the blues singer, killed one, maybe two men. During his last stretch in a Louisiana prison, he used his rough but beguiling voice, his twelve-string guitar, and some improvised lyrics to win a pardon from the governor of the state, thereby gaining enough publicity to launch a concert career.

In 1940 I attended his first performance in

the North. I knew his background and expected a fierce-looking devil to stride onstage. Naturally, his appearance proved to be pleasant and his demeanor, mild. Just the same, I chose to accommodate my expectations with at least one dramatic exposure. While Leadbelly was performing, I manipulated my flashgun to produce the sinister chiaroscuro portrait you see on the previous page.

The "real" Leadbelly can be seen below in a rare pairing with an equally legendary musician, Bunk Johnson.

Bunk and Leadbelly; clarinetist George Lewis, bottom left; bassist Alcide "Slow Drag" Pavageau, rear.

William "Bunk" Johnson

Bunk Johnson was an established New Orleans trumpet player before the turn of the century! For years he did well at his craft. But in 1930, in the depths of the Great Depression, jobs became scarce. His miseries were multiplied by an accident that cost him his horn and, even worse for a trumpet player, his teeth. Discouraged, he quit music and became a field hand in New Iberia, Louisiana.

Many years later he was rediscovered by a jazz historian, Bill Russell. Fans soon came to listen to Bunk as if he were a supposedly extinct creature miraculously found alive. By the middle 1940s, when this photo was taken, he had new teeth and was again a busy musician, though nearly seventy. The young lady with Bunk? His recent bride.

More old-timers came from New Orleans than from any other city. The four shown here were working musicians as far back as 1910 and were still busy through the 1940s!

(RIGHT, ABOVE) *Warren "Baby" Dodds was percussionist at one time or another for many of the top traditional leaders, including King Oliver, Louis Armstrong, Jelly Roll Morton, and Bunk Johnson. His elder brother, Johnny, an influential clarinetist, died in 1940.*

(RIGHT, BELOW) *Albert Nicholas played a classic, supple New Orleans clarinet. He appeared with countless traditional and swing bands; and, like his fellow reed man Sidney Bechet, he was appreciated even more in Europe than in America.*

(BELOW) *George "Pops" Foster was probably the musician most responsible for the tuba's being replaced by the string bass, a far more flexible instrument.*

Sidney Bechet, the eminent soprano saxophonist, was an important jazzman in America, an even more important one in Europe. In 1919, Ernest Ansermet, the Swiss symphony-orchestra conductor, pronounced him a musical giant. In France, Bechet was a national hero; after his death a statue of him was erected on the Riviera.

Those who carefully observed the jazz scene in the '40s might have noticed that the New Orleans style was performed almost entirely by older blacks, never by younger ones. Young blacks wouldn't be caught even listening to it. Those young people who did carry on the New Orleans tradition, both as players and as listeners, were almost invariably white and middle class. It was these same types who also created Dixieland, a style closely related to New Orleans music.

On the East Coast, the most noted of the young white New Orleans practitioners were Bob Wilber's Wildcats, an enthusiastic group first composed mostly of high-school students from Scarsdale, a fashionable suburb of New York City. (On the West Coast, there were the Lu Watters and Turk Murphy bands.) Wilber, a clarinetist and soprano saxophonist, became a live-in disciple of the great traditionalist Sidney Bechet.

The Wildcats, with Bob Wilber, soprano sax; Johnny Glasel, trumpet; Dick Wellstood, piano; Charlie Traeger, bass; and Ed Phyfe, drums.

In the '40s the centers of old-time jazz in New York City, and perhaps the world, were three clubs: Jimmy Ryan's on 52nd Street, Nick's in the Village, and—just a few bars away—Eddie Condon's.

The bands that played those spots were small combos with shifting personnel. Although individuals sometimes became identified with one or another of the clubs, practically every one of these musicians in the course of a couple of years played at least one gig at Ryan's *and* Nick's *and* Condon's.

The music at all three was typically New Orleans or its Dixieland variant; but everything could be heard on occasion, for the instrumentalists were as versatile as they were skillful. Many of them periodically took leave of the New Orleans–Dixieland circuit to work as stars with both swing and sweet bands, as well as with other kinds of musical groups. The last time I saw Jack Lesberg, one of the Condon crew, he was playing bass for a symphony orchestra.

Nick's, with four sizzling favorites: Pee Wee Russell, Muggsy Spanier, Miff Mole, and Joe Grauso.

Jimmy Ryan's—a session featuring Wilbur De Paris, trombone; his brother Sidney, trumpet; Eddie Barefield, clarinet; Charlie Traeger, bass; and Sammy Price, piano.

Francis "Muggsy" Spanier was one of the most sought-after cornetists of the period. With both open horn and plunger mute, he was marvelously full-bodied and precise.

"Pee Wee" Russell had a mournful face, a mumbling voice, and a growling clarinet. But on him it looked good! Pee Wee was one of the best and most loved musicians in jazz.

Eddie Condon

Eddie Condon's, with a typical lineup: (from left) Pee Wee Russell, Max Kaminsky, Wild Bill Davison, Jack Lesberg (rear), George Brunis, Bud Freeman, and Freddie Ohms. Note Eddie Condon's empty chair, in front of Pee Wee.

Eddie Condon's club was newer and shorter-lived than Ryan's or Nick's, but it was the liveliest of the three, thanks largely to its proprietor and permanent floating guitarist, Eddie Condon himself.

Eddie was reputed to be an outstanding musician; he appeared on some historic records and won two *Down Beat* polls. But by the time I got to know him, his best efforts went into promoting music at concerts and at his club, and into playing the role of "a widely quoted personality." (Practically everyone talked about his comment on Hugues Panassie, the French jazz critic who came to the United States and appraised our music: "Who is he to tell us about jazz? We don't tell Frenchmen how to jump on a grape.")

As far as I know, Eddie never took a guitar solo. He stuck to ensemble playing, when he played at all. Often as not, the guitar chair at Condon's was empty. Ever the diligent proprietor, Eddie was frequently off talking with patrons or running quality-control tests at his bar. But his absence didn't matter. The musicians of the day, playing mostly New Orleans and Dixieland standards, could do just fine by themselves.

The Condon crew consisted of twenty-or-so illustrious jazzmen. Some of them are seen on the following pages.

(LEFT, ABOVE) *Lawrence "Bud" Freeman could fit in anywhere. He was at times a sideman with some of the sweetest pop bands, yet at other times was a featured hot soloist with the Benny Goodman and Tommy Dorsey orchestras. The greatest mark of his versatility was being accepted by the Dixielanders; he was the first tenor saxophonist admitted to their ranks.*

(LEFT, BELOW) *Joe Sullivan was the best-known of the Dixieland pianists, but he also was active as an accompanist for singers such as Bing Crosby.*

(BELOW) *George Wettling, though one of the busiest drummers of the era, made time for serious painting. A student of the abstract expressionist Stuart Davis, George hoped his painting would prove as successful as his drumming, but in vain.*

Jack Lesberg, Max Kaminsky, and Michael "Peanuts" Hucko were normally among the more serious of the Condonites. Max played trumpet; Peanuts, clarinet.

George Brunis and Tony Parenti were regulars in the trombone and clarinet chairs at Condon's.

Here are three traditionalists who were not associated with any particular club or other subgroup.

(LEFT, ABOVE) *Joseph "Wingy" Manone, a popular trumpeter and leader, put more effort into playing clown than playing musician, but he could be a fine instrumentalist. Along with Louis Prima, Wingy was the best-known of the white imitators of Louis Armstrong.*

In his role as clown, Wingy played up his homely looks. I went along with him in this close-up, which initially accompanied a newspaper story that began: "A gargoyle broke off from the back wall of Town Hall and walked towards me. It was Wingy Manone. . . ."

(LEFT, BELOW) *Art Hodes was for a time just another good piano player. He became well known by crusading for old-time jazz. Hodes pushed his cause by organizing various traditional-style combos and by touting New Orleans and Dixieland music while working as a radio disc-jockey and as a magazine writer.*

(BELOW) *Milton "Mezz" Mezzrow, like Hodes, had more significance as a crusader for traditional jazz than as a musician. He was also an active promoter of black culture and called himself a "voluntary Negro." His book,* Really the Blues, *was one of the first and best of many autobiographies by jazzmen.*

2. SATCHMO AND THE DUKE: BEYOND CATEGORY

During the Golden Age of Jazz, a cornet-shaped cornucopia spilled forth a marvelous abundance of music makers: Basie, Fitzgerald, Gillespie, Goodman, Hawkins, Hines, Holiday, Lunceford, Parker, Shaw, Tatum, Teagarden, Young . . . and more. Giants, all. Still, there were two others who towered above them: Daniel Louis Armstrong and Edward Kennedy Ellington—Satchmo and the Duke.

Satchmo and the Duke: one, the greatest instrumentalist in the history of hot music; the other, the foremost creator of orchestral jazz. One, raised in a New Orleans slum and in a home for delinquents; the other, raised in a middle-class Washington environment and so pampered by his family that "I must have been six years old before my feet touched the ground."

Famous as far back as the '20s, Satchmo and the Duke can scarcely be considered products of the Golden Age. Still, throughout the '30s and '40s they loomed above the entire jazz scene. With audiences, they were more popular and respected than ever; with musicians (except for the most sacrilegious of the young-bloods), they continued to be the idols venerated above all others. Clearly, Satchmo and the Duke are as much a part of the Golden Age as of any other jazz era. They cannot be narrowly classified. They are beyond time . . . and beyond category.

Louis "Satchmo" Armstrong

It's difficult to think jazz without thinking Armstrong. Almost from that moment in 1922 when young Louis left New Orleans to join King Oliver in Chicago, his electrifying technique and direct emotional intensity overwhelmed the jazz world. Thousands of cornet and trumpet players adopted his way of playing as best they could. Equal numbers of trombonists, saxophonists, and piano players adapted their attack to resemble his.

Then there's Satchmo's singing. His voice was hoarse, gutteral, totally unmusical by conventional standards; but by transferring his phrasing and feelings from horn to voice, he became the best of jazz vocalists. Many imitators followed, even when it meant masking a legitimate voice-box to affect one lined with gravel.

During much of the Golden Age, Louis Armstrong shifted from serious musician to amusing entertainer. He clowned . . . showed off spectacular high notes . . . sang sticky pop songs . . . became a movie star. But he never

35

could completely conceal his musical talent. Satchmo's most banal performances were peppered with flecks of his genius.

Despite his lofty perch, Satch was easily approached and as genial offstage as on. Almost everyone with whom he had much contact regarded this open, earthy man as a friend, even though he often couldn't remember names and called most everyone Pops. (In turn, almost everyone called *him* Pops, though he also answered to Louis, Satch, and Satchmo —the last two being diminutives of Satchelmouth.)

Satch, like so many ordinary humans, had a weight problem and had both fat periods and lean. As a prodigious consumer of red beans and rice (he often ended his many amusing letters with "Red beans and ricely yours"), Louis was more often fat than lean.

Louis had a personal diet that he touted. It was heavy on Pluto Water, a patented laxa-

tive that was popular years ago. Genial Satch kept in his inside jacket pocket copies of the diet, which he liked to hand out to friends who he thought needed it.

Louis and I happened to have the same dentist. A few months before Louis died, I found him entering the dentist's office as I was about to leave. The great man's famous chops were hurting and, from the way he looked, so were many other parts of him.

Bad as Satch must have felt, he was his usual gracious self. We chatted about old times until it was time for me to depart. Just before I was about to disappear through the door, he called out, "Hey, Pops, wait!" I turned toward him and could see that he had been sizing up my hulk. He then pulled a sheet of paper from his inside jacket pocket and handed it to me. "There's this diet, man. The greatest. Try it."

And I might have. But I just couldn't find a store that still sold Pluto Water.

By 1929 Louis Armstrong, already world famous, had given up playing the small-combo jazz that had been so musically rewarding. Instead he became, in effect, a solo entertainer. There continued to be Armstrong orchestras, but they were really the bands of others that Louis merely fronted. The sidemen kept in the background while Louis did his thing, projecting his fabulous personality more than his fabulous music.

Then in the mid-'40s Satch formed a small group of all-stars; he returned to the format that had first brought him fame. Once again the jazz poured out, although Satch still managed to get in some clowning, make some movies, and come up with smash-hit pop records like "Mack the Knife" and "Hello, Dolly."

The photographs on these and the next few pages show some of the later-day stars who were associated with Armstrong.

At this concert in New York's Town Hall, Louis' group consisted of Jack Teagarden, trombone; Bobby Hackett, trumpet; Peanuts Hucko, clarinet; Bob Haggart, bass; Sid Catlett, drums; and Dick Cary, piano.

Earl "Fatha" Hines played piano with Louis Armstrong for several years in the late 1940s.
More significantly, Fatha worked with Satch back in 1927, when, reacting to Louis' blazing
talent, he revolutionized jazz piano playing by using his right hand to play trumpet-style,
single-note lines in the Armstrong manner. For the next two decades, almost every young
piano player—most notably, Teddy Wilson—fell into Fatha's groove.
   During part of the Golden Age, Fatha was a bandleader and the composer of such music as
"Rosetta," his theme song. He also established a reputation for encouraging young musicians;
at one time his band included Dizzy Gillespie, Charlie Parker, Sarah Vaughan, and Billy
Eckstine.

(RIGHT, TOP) *Henry "Red" Allen, a trumpeter with a slashing, raucous attack, led his own small group through much of the '40s, but frequently backed Satchmo, especially on concert dates.*

(RIGHT, CENTER) *Jack "Jay C." Higginbotham was a trombonist with a powerful drive. He was a perfect match for Red Allen, with whom he was frequently teamed. For several years Jay C. was one of Armstrong's regulars, often alongside Red.*

(RIGHT, BOTTOM) *Sidney "Big Sid" Catlett, long an Armstrong stalwart, was a gifted and versatile drummer. He was one of the few "older" swing percussionists who easily made the transition to bop.*

(BELOW) *Arthur "Zutty" Singleton was a member of Armstrong's early, legendary Hot Five recording group, as well as more recent Armstrong combos.*

Weldon J. "Jack" Teagarden was the preeminent trombonist of the Golden Age. After giving up his own band, he began a long association with Armstrong. Like Satch, Jack sang jazz almost as well as he played it. On vocal duets his soft, lazy Texan drawl proved an ideal complement to Satch's robust growling.

(OPPOSITE) *Duke in a backstage dressing room.*

Edward Kennedy "Duke" Ellington

I was always awed by Duke Ellington. Everything about him dazzled me: his music, of course; but also his energy, his hipness, his suavity. Even his physical appearance. Like Satchmo, Duke eventually acquired an over-ample waistline, which first became apparent to me when I interviewed him in a backstage dressing room after he had showered. Yet minutes later, when he went onstage to perform, he was transformed. He had taken on the dapper look that was an Ellington trademark. The change was due partly to his expensive, well-tailored suit (one of more than a dozen that he always took with him), but what really

made the difference was the special magic that was in him and that he could, at will, infuse into his bearing.

Ellington's magic filled his music, too. As a writer of popular tunes, he turned out such superior hits as "Mood Indigo," "Solitude," "Sophisticated Lady," "In a Sentimental Mood," "I Got It Bad and That Ain't Good," and "Satin Doll." As a piano player, Duke was something less than spectacular. But his playing was just right for the orchestral role he assigned to the keyboard. Which brings us to the orchestra itself. . . . The Duke's instrument was acknowledged to be not so much the piano as the orchestra. He was an instrumentalist who "played a band." And what a player! With his band Duke created jazz that had more colors, more textures, more surprises than any other jazz group.

Still, the Ellington orchestra was not everybody's favorite. Some listeners found its music too exotic and convoluted. Even some Ellington partisans conceded that for pure, exuberant, driving jazz, Duke's band couldn't match Count Basie's. That's not to say that the Ellingtonians lacked a strong pulse. One of Duke's hit tunes was "It Don't Mean a Thing If It Ain't Got That Swing"; Ellington rarely ignored its message.

Sometimes the Duke's "serious" concert and religious music did become a bit pretentious, with only a muted jazz feeling; but at all other times Ellington kept in the groove, and he did so year after year.

I particularly remember 1940, when an amazing cluster of Ellington instrumental sides were issued on Victor records: "Jack the Bear," "Harlem Air Shaft," "Concerto for Cootie," "Ko-Ko," "Warm Valley," "Cotton Tail," and "Never No Lament." (Later, "Concerto for Cootie" and "Never No Lament" were given lyrics and became pop hits under

Duke in 1939.

the titles "Do Nothing Till You Hear From Me" and "Don't Get Around Much Any More.") Many critics now recognize these re-cordings as the greatest concentration of masterpieces in jazz history.

When those 1940 sides first appeared, I gave them good reviews, but never realized just how high a musical peak they had reached. That's one of the problems of listening to genius: it's so easy to take even masterpieces for granted!

Duke and the author in the author's Washington home, 1941. With them are, at left, Ahmet Ertegun and, at right, his brother, Nesuhi. The Erteguns were jazz fans and the sons of the Turkish Ambassador to the United States. Today they are major powers in the music industry: Ahmet is the head of Atlantic Records; Nesuhi, the head of WEA (Warner-Electra-Atlantic International). They are also, respectively, the president and chairman of the Cosmos soccer team.

The French-Gypsy guitarist Django Reinhardt backstage with part of the Ellington orchestra during a joint concert tour. From left: Al Sears, Shelton Hemphill, Junior Raglin, Reinhardt, Lawrence Brown, Harry Carney, and Johnny Hodges.

During the Golden Age, playing with the Duke Ellington orchestra was the ultimate goal of just about every black musician. Being tapped by His Highness the Duke meant being recognized as one of the world's outstanding instrumentalists. It was like getting a Pulitzer Prize.

Among other dividends for Ellington sidemen was the special attention they received; the band's arrangements were written with specific players in mind. Although each of Duke's musicians had to subordinate himself to some extent to the Ellington style, he was still given an extraordinary opportunity to show off his talents, thanks to those tailor-made charts.

With benefits like these, musicians did their best not only to get into the orchestra but to stay in. Leaving the Duke voluntarily, at least during the Golden Age, was almost unthinkable, and personnel changes were rare. When, late in 1940, Cootie Williams quit to go with Benny Goodman for more money, it was such a shocker that the Raymond Scott orchestra immortalized it with a recording, "When Cootie Left the Duke."

Whitney Balliett, who covers jazz for *The New Yorker*, describes the interrelationship between the Duke and his men: "Hodges or Bigard or Ben Webster would give him eight or twelve beautiful bars and those would pass through his extraordinary head and come out as 'Mood Indigo' or 'Sophisticated Lady. . . .' The Ellington afflatus was dangerous. It drained his musicians, and at the same time, because so many of his tunes were written specifically for them, it spoiled them. When longtime sidemen left, they either dropped into obscurity or, thirsting for the Master's attention, returned to the fold."

Shown on these pages are many of the more prominent Ellingtonians who were in the fold during the Golden Age.

William "Cat" Anderson was the band's high-note specialist. When he was about to screech one, he liked to point out where the note would go.

John "Rabbit" Hodges had a completely deadpan expression, yet out of his horn came the most sensuous, most voluptuous sounds in jazz. Almost all of Johnny's career was spent in Duke's reed section, although he formed his own band for a while, taking along another Ellingtonian, tenor man Al Sears (background), as musical director.

William "Sonny" Greer
joined forces with Duke in
1919, in Washington: two
sharp young cats out to
show the world their stuff.

Ray Nance, ever the
entertainer, jived around
doing his thing as singer,
dancer, and trumpeter. But
when he came to grips
with his violin, he became
serious. Suddenly the jive
was gone.

SATCHMO AND THE DUKE: BEYOND CATEGORY 47

Harry Carney joined Ellington when he was only 16 years old and remained with the band until his death more than 47 years later! He was for a long time the only great baritone saxophonist in jazz. The hot harpist in this jam session was Adele Girard.

William "Swee' Pea" Strayhorn was only 23 when he was brought into the band to back up Ellington as arranger and pianist. He successfully met this formidable challenge and went on to become Duke's alter ego. Strayhorn's creative output became almost indistinguishable from the boss's. "Take the 'A' Train," a Swee' Pea composition that sounded "all Ellington," emerged as the band's theme song.

(ABOVE LEFT) *Ben Webster was the first tenor sax player to be featured by Duke. His driving Kansas City horn added a new sound to the band. Starting with "Cotton Tail," Ellington regularly wrote music that displayed Ben's exciting tenor.*

(ABOVE RIGHT) *Rex Stewart, an amusing and intelligent fellow, frequently expressed himself with witty cornet playing. In "Boy Meets Horn" Rex created a novel and much-imitated "squeezed" tone by depressing his cornet valves only halfway.*

(RIGHT) *Charles "Cootie" Williams was the Ellington superstar whose growling trumpet provided much of the "jungle" sound that the band often featured. I once asked Cootie how he came by his famous growl. I was hoping he'd reveal some profound motivations, something about deep-rooted social torments pouring out of his horn. "Well," Cootie answered, "I was hired by Duke to take Bubber Miley's place, and Duke told me, 'Growl like Bubber.' So I growled."*

Barney Bigard, who had played with King Oliver, added his fluid New Orleans clarinet to the Ellington palette. Barney's swooping lines became one of the band's most distinctive sounds.

Evans "Tyree" Glenn, an Ellingtonian for five years, had an odd double specialty: trombone and vibes. Versatile Tyree was also an actor, on the side.

3. SWING AND THE BIRTH OF THE GOLDEN AGE

The Golden Age of Jazz, like most eras, came in slowly, almost imperceptibly. Then suddenly the world took notice. It was here!

Some say its ultimate arrival can be pinpointed to that day in the summer of 1935 when the Benny Goodman orchestra, after a dismal series of unsuccessful cross-country one-nighters, arrived at the Palomar Ballroom in Los Angeles. To its surprise, the band was greeted hysterically by an overflow crowd of young people!

The Los Angeles audience had been prepared for the Goodman style. They had been listening to Benny's band on a network show called "Let's Dance," and the music had grabbed them but good. When they finally heard the music at first hand, boom! An explosion.

Why, until then, had the band's tour flopped? Because of time-zone differences, the "Let's Dance" program reached the East and the Middle West at too late an hour to be heard by the young people of those regions; hence their failure to respond as the Westerners did to the band's personal appearance. However, within a year of the Palomar date, jazz, under the name of "swing," had overwhelmed every part of the country.

Jazz had, of course, been with us long before Goodman's triumph, but it was largely confined to special groups: blacks, a few white musicians, some white fans, and a handful of critics, nearly all of them European. (Jazz had a special fascination for European intellectuals.)

As for the so-called Jazz Age of the '20s . . . that title was a musical misnomer. The "jazz" that most Americans heard at that time was usually not the real thing. Paul Whiteman, then the "King of Jazz," played virtually none of it. Al Jolson, the popular Jazz Singer, sang literally none of it.

But underground at least, the number of true believers was growing. By the time Benny Goodman came on the scene, a considerable amount of authentic hot music was being played. There were notable black orchestras like those of Duke Ellington, Louis Armstrong, Jimmie Lunceford, Fletcher Henderson, and Bennie Moten. There were or had recently been fairly good white bands, too, like those of Ben Pollack, Red Nichols, Ray Noble, and Glen Gray.

Bit by bit, real jazz began creeping into the consciousness of typical young Americans. By 1935 they were just about ready for it. Then Benny hit Palomar and, at last, *it arrived!*

Benny Goodman

Benny Goodman was the right man at the right time. A superlative musician with glittering improvisational techniques, he was also a relentlessly ambitious careerist who probed in many directions, searching for avenues to success. Through fortuitous timing, he found the right one.

His great good fortune was using jazz as his vehicle. It was a bandwagon that millions were just ready to board. "He was," writes critic Leonard Feather in his *Encyclopedia of Jazz*, "the first to adopt an uncompromising jazz style, one that took both standard and popular material and turned it into the idiom that became known as swing, thus starting an entire new era."

Here are some of his other successes:

He made the clarinet, at least for a while, one of the most popular of instruments.

He hired dozens of superb but unknown musicians, gaining for them the attention they deserved.

He popularized chamber jazz by featuring instrumental trios and other small units.

And he employed a number of blacks, using his prestige to break down racial taboos so that the mixing of black and white musicians became possible and even commonplace.

A dazzling list of accomplishments!

Benny Goodman was surely a tower in the world of jazz, but he was also a terror among those with whom he worked. He was constantly accused of being cold, insensitive, thoughtless. He tended to ignore his sidemen for long periods; then the moment he disapproved of their playing, he'd shoot them down with the awesome stare known as The Ray.

Understandably, there was a high turnover rate in the Goodman orchestra. For a long time the gag line on 52nd Street was that at any one time there were three Goodman orchestras: the one he had just fired, the one he had just hired, and the one that was still with him.

Many of Benny's detractors maintained that much of Benny's glory rightfully belonged to socialite John Hammond, a socially conscious jazz devotee who frequently gave advice to Benny. John was undoubtedly responsible for many of Benny's "discoveries," as well as for getting Benny to hire blacks. (Hammond, often working in unofficial capacities, also played crucial roles in building the careers of a dozen other top stars, from Count Basie and Billie Holiday to Bob Dylan and Bruce Springsteen.)

It was Hammond who, in 1935, persuaded Gene Krupa to join Benny's band. In his autobiography, *John Hammond on Record*, John tells how he had to twist Gene's arm—hard—to get him to come, for Krupa had already had experience with Goodman and didn't want more of same. Gene relented and joined Benny, but he could never do more than tolerate his boss. Still, Gene, like other ex-Goodman sidemen, had to admit that, personal issues aside, Benny was a great benefactor of music.

Nat Shapiro and Nat Hentoff, in their book, *Hear Me Talkin to Ya*, have this quotation from Krupa: "Benny built himself a band playing musicians' music. . . . It allowed us to play the way we honestly wanted to play, with good pay and before huge, appreciative audiences. In the days before the Goodman era, we played that way, too, but in smaller bands and with no similar success. . . . For all that Benny did for music, for jazz, for musicians, and for me, I, for one, doff my cap in a salute of sincere appreciation."

In my own encounters with Benny, he followed form. Although he never shot me with The Ray, he never exactly exuded charm, either. In each interview he answered questions with as few syllables as possible: a couple of "no's," a "yes" or two, several grunts, and here and there some short sentences. For lack of verbal tinder, the interviews quickly burned out.

But, as Gene Krupa said, for all he's done for jazz, I doff my hat in sincere appreciation.

Benny on the bandstand with saxophonist Vido Musso and drummer Sid Catlett.

Goodman was the first important jazz musician to play straight classical music in public. It was an interesting venture but not very successful artistically or financially. Here he's rehearsing for a concert conducted by Leonard Bernstein.

Dozens of outstanding musicians passed in and out of the Benny Goodman orchestra. The BG alumni association became one of the most distinguished societies in the music world, with many of its members moving up to lead orchestras of their own.

The most successful of the ex-Goodman sidemen were Gene Krupa, Harry James, and Lionel Hampton. For much of the Golden Age each was the most popular musician on his respective instrument, and the orchestras they led sometimes challenged that of Benny, himself.

Gene Krupa

Harry James

Lionel Hampton. Hamp's supercharged energies and blazing talents catapulted him to stardom. His specialty was vibes, but he also played flashy drums and piano. On piano, he used only his index fingers, flailing them like vibraphone mallets. (A second pianist usually filled in the "left hand" parts.)

(ABOVE) *Teddy Wilson, an impeccable pianist, was the first black musician hired by Goodman and the outstanding keyboard man playing in the Earl Hines tradition. Teddy is at left, drummer Zutty Singleton at right.*

(ABOVE LEFT) *Jess Stacy was another of Benny's fine pianists. He played with the full band, while Teddy was featured with the Trio and Quartet.*

(BELOW LEFT) *Melvin "Mel" Powell, a notable piano player who joined Benny in 1941, is shown with his wife, actress Martha Scott.*

William "Count" Basie

For those who liked their swing direct and to the point, the greatest of the bands belonged to Count Basie. John S. Wilson, jazz critic of *The New York Times*, put it this way: "At the height of the Swing Era, this was the swing band incarnate."

Count Basie and his musicians generated a powerful drive that used crescendos of riffs interspersed with blazing solos, all of it further propelled by the best rhythm section in the business. It was a comparatively uncomplicated style, but it was irresistibly compelling . . . and glorious.

In the midst of all this throbbing, unfettered power, the Count's own playing seemed anomalous—delicate, sparse, completely understated. Yet it was perfectly suited for its job. His keyboard notes may have been economical in number, but each was exquisitely timed to give a subtle but unmistakable rhythmic kick that spurred the other musicians.

One week late in 1938, both the Count

Count Basie, Ray Bauduc, Bob Haggart, and Herschel Evans on the stage of the Howard. Bauduc and Haggart had only recently recorded their famous drum-bass duet, "Big Noise from Winnetka." Evans, a highly regarded tenor man, was to die only a few months later, at 30, becoming an instant legend.

An incongruous but sensational reed section: Herschel Evans, Eddie Miller, Lester Young, and Matty Matlock.

Basie and the Bob Crosby orchestras were in Washington. I was able to obtain the use of the Howard Theater stage "after hours" and persuaded both groups to come together for a jam session. There was just one problem—the Crosby band played Dixieland, a style as far from that of the Basie band as it was possible to get and still be jazz. Could they fit together musically? They could. Their differences were insignificant compared with their fundamental similarities. That evening, fantastic music was made.

During its long history the Count Basie orchestra went through several distinct periods. Each could claim a number of musical stars. Here are pictures of some of them.

Lester "Pres" Young was the most distinguished and influential of Basie's many fine sidemen. When playing, Lester was easily recognizable, even from the rear, because of the novel way he held his horn. More important was the novel way he played his horn; it turned around the sax men of the next generation. (The small photo shows Pres from the front.)

Oran "Lips" Page, shown here sitting in with Sidney Bechet, played with the Basie band in its Kansas City days. He then went on to spark other groups, including his own. Back, left: Freddie Moore; back, right: Lloyd Phillips.

Wilbur "Buck" Clayton, trumpeter and arranger, was featured on most of Basie's best-known recordings. When this photo was taken, he had left the Count to lead his own group. Ted Kelly is on trombone; Ken Kersey on piano; Benny Fonville on bass; Scoville Brown on clarinet; and Shep Shepherd on drums. Kersey was an early bop man.

William "Dickie" Wells (with the mute) and Henry "Benny" Morton, both veteran jazzmen, were the trombone soloists during Basie's early "glory" years.

James Melvin "Jimmie" Lunceford

For several years, beginning in 1934, Jimmie Lunceford had the band with the biggest beat in the business. Much of the credit belonged to the distinctive arrangements of trumpeter Sy Oliver and pianist Ed Wilcox, together with the musicianship of many outstanding sidemen. In the middle '40s most of the key musicians left and the band declined. Jimmie himself died in 1947.

(OPPOSITE) *Jimmie Lunceford "all alone,"*
soon after several key sidemen had left him.

(BELOW) *The pulsating power of the*
Lunceford orchestra was particularly apparent
in "battles of swing." In one contest, at which
I officiated, the Krupa band, which by itself
seemed so solid, sounded thin and tinny when
juxtaposed with the Lunceford band. Shown
here are Lunceford, the author, and Krupa.

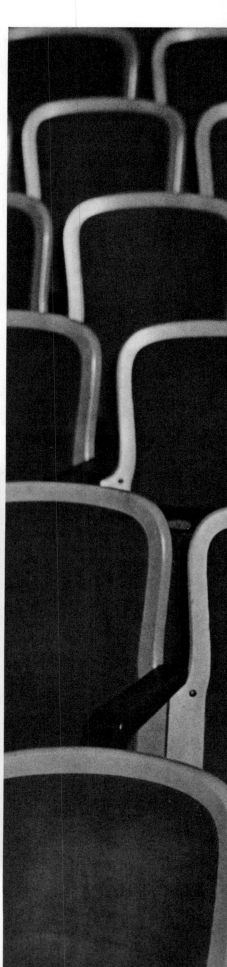

Sy Oliver, whose arrangements set the style for the Lunceford band, later did the same for Tommy Dorsey.

James "Trummy" Young. His out-of-breath singing style and robust trombone were strong points in the Lunceford band.

Willie Smith, alto sax, was the outstanding instrumentalist in the Lunceford organization. He's shown here on a post-Lunceford recording date. The trombonist is Juan Tizol, who had recently left Duke Ellington.

Joe Thomas and Ed Wilcox took over the Lunceford band after Jimmie's death, but without much success. In this rehearsal shot Ed is at the piano, Joe on tenor, and Omer Simeon on alto.

John Kirby

The first important chamber-jazz group of the Golden Age was the John Kirby Sextet. It had light, tightly scored arrangements, but still managed to swing. Kirby's wife, popular Maxine Sullivan, became famous recording "Loch Lomond" with Claude Thornhill, before joining Kirby. Some of the Kirby personnel are shown here.

Billy Kyle

William "Buster" Bailey

Charlie Shavers

Russell Procope

Maxine Sullivan

During the Golden Age of Jazz there were several popular swing bands that played hot music at least an appreciable part of the time. Here are some of their leaders.

(OPPOSITE) *Kenneth "Red" Norvo was considered by many to be the subtlest of jazz musicians. His delicate, swinging style on vibraharp and xylophone was much admired by fellow musicians and discerning listeners. He led a series of small combos that reflected his exquisite touch.*

(BELOW LEFT) *Charlie Barnet was a worshipful Duke Ellington fan. His band often played in the Ellington tradition and sometimes used Ellington alumni. Charlie's was the most racially integrated of the big bands.*

(BELOW RIGHT) *Artie Shaw, with both his superb orchestra and his brilliant clarinet playing, for a while eclipsed Benny Goodman in popularity polls. A volatile artist, he kept abandoning and reentering music, finally quitting for good to become a writer. (Artie always admired writers and literature. I'll never forget the specially made "one-shelf" leather bookcase he carried around, even on one-nighters.) The shadowy portrait of him was originally used for a story that described his being half in, half out of music.*

Equally volatile in his love life, Artie was married at least seven times. His wives were spectacular women and included Lana Turner, Ava Gardner, Betty Kern (Jerome Kern's daughter), and Kathleen Winsor, author of Forever Amber.

Woodrow "Woody"
Herman had several first-
rate orchestras. The first
one featured the blues, a
style with which his own
playing and singing were
most comfortable.
Successive "Herman
Herds" became
progressively more modern.

Bennett "Benny" Carter
was probably the most
versatile of all topflight
jazz musicians. He was
best known for his alto sax,
but he was gifted, too, with
trumpet, tenor, and
clarinet, besides being a
superb arranger. His
orchestra never received
the popularity it deserved.

Bernard "Buddy" Rich was a spectacular jazz musician and showman. Besides his rapid-fire drumming, he sang and danced, never failing to build up a storm wherever he performed.

Tommy Dorsey was one of the best-known orchestra leaders of the swing era. (His brother, Jimmy, had a popular band, too.) Many outstanding musicians and singers worked for him, including Frank Sinatra, who gained fame with Tommy and developed much of his singing technique by listening to Tommy's smooth, legato-style trombone.

When the big-band business slumped, Tommy tried a stint as a disc-jockey. At his opening, he interviewed singer Beryl Davis. In the background you may be able to spot Georgie Auld, Ray McKinley, Mary Lou Williams, and Josh White.

Cabell "Cab" Calloway was a novelty singer rather than a jazzman. (I can remember a recording date where he had a terrible time coming in on the right beat.) But he had many outstanding sidemen, all of whom got valuable exposure backing Cab's sensational personality.

Machito had a superb Latin band that was very much part of the jazz scene, with American sidemen freely intermixing with Cubans and Puerto Ricans. Here Machito is playing maracas, with the rest of his rhythm section joining in.

Louis Jordan and his Tympany Five was one of a number of small, good bands that specialized in novelties. The group had many smash hits, including "Knock Me a Kiss" and "Gonna Move to the Outskirts of Town." Louis was not only a witty showman but also an excellent musician; he first gained prominence as the alto star of the Chick Webb Orchestra.

Glen "Spike" Gray, leader of the Casa Loma orchestra, led the first big white orchestra that attempted to play real jazz. Its stiff arrangements didn't quite make it, musically; but the group was popular and did much to prepare an audience for Benny Goodman and other succeeding swing bands. (Note the hand-gun on Spike's dressing table.)

76 THE GOLDEN AGE OF JAZZ

Claude Thornhill and Ray McKinley. There were dozens of swing bands in the '30s and '40s that were on the border of hot music. Many of their instrumentalists could take off with first-rate solos, and the general level of musicianship was high; but their overall output was too "pop" to qualify as jazz. Two of the best representatives of this group were the bands of Claude Thornhill, who introduced French horns and other enrichments to the swing scene, and Ray McKinley, one of several leaders who at one time or another led the Glenn Miller orchestra after Miller's death in Europe while on military duty.

A single new York City block—52nd Street between Fifth and Sixth Avenues—was the very center of the jazz world during much of the Golden Age. The ground floors of the brownstone houses that lined The Street were jammed with night clubs, some featuring girlie shows and comedians but most specializing in hot music. There were the Onyx, the 3 Deuces, Downbeat, the Famous Door, Jimmy Ryan's, Kelly's Stable, and—nearby—the Hickory House.

For a decade The Street was heaven on earth to jazz fans. They formed a peripatetic audience, strolling from club to club to check out the living legends performing on any given night. The block was probably the liveliest spot in New York. But by the end of the '40s, The Street was dead. It was unable to withstand three converging forces: an economic recession in the music business; the degrading influx of hordes of dope pushers; and the inexorable encroachment of Rockefeller Center, which alone ensured The Street's demise.

The Street was great while it lasted. The next few pages show some of the celebrated musicians who appeared on this fabled block.

Art Tatum was the piano players' favorite piano player. Though legally blind, he covered the keyboard with awesome speed, while creating fantastic harmonic improvisations. Some critics said his prodigious embellishments destroyed the jazz structure of his music. But pianists were overwhelmed by him. When Tatum entered a room, more than one of them had been known to whisper, "God is in the house!"

Mary Lou Williams, the first woman to attain top-level stature in jazz, became famous as the pianist-arranger of the Andy Kirk band from Kansas City. Afterward she worked mostly with her own trio or as a single, more often in the Village than on 52nd Street.

Erroll Garner was a 52nd Street regular. His unconventional but pleasing jazz piano was a sure draw at the clubs. On records he was the best-seller among jazz pianists.

(OPPOSITE) Nat "King" Cole with his famous trio. At first Nat was primarily an instrumentalist and won polls as the country's best jazz piano player. It wasn't until later that he became a top-selling singer.

(RIGHT) Dave Tough, considered by a great many musicians to be the best of the jazz drummers, was also exceptionally bright, wrote well, and could be a probing conversationalist. Despite his abilities, he was hopelessly melancholic, with a gaunt visage that matched his mournful personality.

Dave was never satisfied. Between sets on club gigs, this supreme drummer often felt obliged to go to the cellar to work out on a practice pad! That's what he was doing when this shot was taken.

(BELOW) Boogie-woogie piano was a craze in the early '40s. Its most prominent artists were Meade Lux Lewis, Albert Ammons, and shown here, Pete Johnson.

(ABOVE LEFT) *Carl Kress, besides being an outstanding guitarist, had a special distinction: he was co-owner of the original Onyx Club, probably the most famous of the 52nd Street jazz spots.*

(ABOVE RIGHT) *Al Hall, a sound, adaptable bassist, played everything from big-band jazz to theater music and even had his own jazz record company.*

(LEFT) *William "Cozy" Cole could fit in with any style. He was a drummer for New Orleans bands, for boppers, and for everything in between.*

(OPPOSITE) *Leroy "Slam" Stewart hit it big with Slim Gaillard (Slim and Slam) on "Flat Foot Floogie." He was later part of the Art Tatum trio. Slam's playing was easily recognized; on solos, he hummed in unison with his bowing.*

(OPPOSITE) *Coleman "Bean" Hawkins, the greatest virtuoso of the tenor sax during the Golden Age, is one of a handful of jazz supermen. His version of "Body and Soul" became a universal jazz anthem.*

(LEFT, ABOVE) *Al Casey, shown on guitar with drummer Denzil Best and bassist John Levy, was long a mainstay with Fats Waller's combo. After Fats's death, Al worked with other small groups, usually as leader.*

(LEFT, BELOW) *Joe Marsala, a fine clarinet and sax man, had a combo that played periodically at the Hickory House, a half-block west of the main part of The Street. His band usually included brother Marty, who was an excellent trumpet player, and Joe's wife, Adele Girard, who startled audiences with her hot harp and pretty face.*

(BELOW) *Jean Baptiste "Django" Reinhardt was not one of the 52nd Streeters, nor—except for a brief tour with Duke Ellington—was he ever part of the American scene. For that matter, it isn't even certain that he should be considered a real jazz guitarist. But, no matter. The jazz world embraced this French Gypsy for his role with the Quintet of the Hot Club of France, whose unique recordings influenced many American jazz instrumentalists. Two of Django's fingers (note the scars) became useless when they were burned in a Gypsy caravan fire, which partly accounted for his unusual technique.*

Eugene "Honey Bear" Sedric, a first-rate clarinet and tenor, was for a long time the man who "ran" Fats Waller's band. In the large photo, I made him look as close to a honey bear as I could. The small photo shows what he was really like.

Sol Yaged, a symphony man turned jazzman, idolized Benny Goodman and liked to talk about him, as well as play like him. Some say he even got to look like BG. With Sol in this photo are bassist John Levy and pianist Jimmy Jones.

(RIGHT) *Bill Coleman, a sensitive, swinging horn man, was much admired by fellow musicians, but found a large, appreciative audience only in France.*

(BELOW LEFT) *Illinois Jacquet started a trend among tenor sax players with his boisterous honking on Lionel Hampton's "Flying Home." He later became a star with the Jazz at the Philharmonic group.*

(BELOW RIGHT) *Arnett Cobb replaced Illinois Jacquet in the Hampton band, delivering frenzied Jacquet-style blowing. Here the "World's Wildest Tenor Man" is with his own band. Arnett personally preferred playing in a warm, contemplative manner—as did Illinois. But it was better business to blow crazy.*

Roy "Little Jazz" Eldridge
was a much-imitated
trumpeter. He starred with
Gene Krupa, Artie Shaw,
and Fletcher Henderson,
as well as with his own
band. Roy was the most
influential musician on his
instrument between the
reigns of Louis Armstrong
and Dizzy Gillespie.

Billy Butterfield played
clean, melodic trumpet
much like Hackett's. He
was in demand both with
swing bands and with
studio orchestras.

Bobby Hackett was the most melodic of the jazz trumpet men. When comedian Jackie Gleason chose to make records featuring "pretty" but skillfully played music, he picked Bobby to be the organizer and star of the "Gleason band."

Robert "Jonah" Jones, a personable trumpet player, became well known working with violinist Stuff Smith. Before he formed his own orchestra, his horn and voice were featured in various big-name bands. (The "directing" arm in this shot belongs to Cab Calloway.)

Hezekiah "Stuff" Smith. There are few violins in jazz; but Stuff, using his own homemade techniques, extracted from this refined instrument a stream of witty and rollicking hot phrases. More of same came from his pungent voice.

Eddie South, a classically trained musician, played a more orthodox violin than did Stuff Smith, but his fiddling nonetheless ended up . . . jazz.

Musicians in the '40s who found themselves temporarily out of work were able to keep "with it" by practicing at sessions conducted by Jacob "Brick" Fleagle, a guitarist and arranger who led a constantly changing, no-name band at Nola's rehearsal studios, on Broadway. Some days the band was a wild sight, with maybe four basses and perhaps enough brass for the gates of heaven.

In this photo Brick (with hat) has several top jazzmen in attendance: to his left, trumpeter and close friend Rex Stewart; to Brick's right, with bow tie, trumpeter Pee Wee Erwin; and, below Pee Wee, trombonist Sandy Williams.

A jam session, with Art
Hodes and Pete Johnson
sharing the piano; Red
Allen, trumpet; Lou
McGarity, trombone; and
Lester Young, with
typically twisted stance,
tenor sax.

Adrian Rollini has a niche
in jazz history as the first
person to swing with a bass
sax. He was also one of the
first to use a vibraphone.

4. THE VOCALISTS

The distinction between music that qualifies as jazz and that which doesn't is often subtle enough to be beyond words or metronomic measurement. The growling trumpet of Cootie Williams, for instance, is "the real thing," while the growling trumpet of Clyde McCoy is "corny"; but exactly what makes them so different? It's hard to explain, though undeniably true.

Assigning vocalists to either jazz or non-jazz categories is especially difficult. What do we do with Nat Cole, an acknowledged master at the piano, who brought much of his jazz sense to his singing but used it on pop ballads and novelties? And how about Billy Eckstine, who sang a lot of *schmaltz* but nonetheless won the respect of most jazz musicians? (Could he have been in a state of grace because he hired a great many outstanding jazzmen?) Nor is it easy to explain why Mildred Bailey, with her gently swinging voice, was emphatically "in," whereas a strongly rhythmic singer like Doris Day was "out." (Did the kind of musicians with whom they associated make a difference?)

And where does this leave Frank Sinatra, who may be the finest vocalist America has produced, but who was generally ignored by the arbiters of hipness?

The author, for one, is not always sure who among the vocalists belongs in this book. Just the same, here are some of the better ones with whom I came in contact during the Golden Age, be they purveyors of 100 percent jazz or only of diluted stuff.

Billie Holiday

The haunting, anguished voice of Billie Holiday, "Lady Day," is one of the glories of music; so I was fortunate to have heard her in the late 1930s and early '40s when she was at her peak.

Billie was a natural. While still a teenager, she stunned nearly every jazz musician and fan who had the chance to catch her heart-wrenching vocals. Billie was only eighteen when she made her first recordings—with no one less than Benny Goodman. By twenty-five, she had become the featured vocalist first with Count Basie, later with Artie Shaw. By then she had also, under her own name and that of Teddy Wilson, made some of the most memorable jazz recordings of all time, using as sidemen an astounding list of instrumen-

talists, including Lester Young. (It was Lester who gave Billie the nickname "Lady Day.")

By the late 1940s everything had changed for Billie. She had been busted on drug charges and consequently had lost the performer's license necessary for working the clubs in New York City. Eventually, after persistent petitioning by her friends, the license was restored and she landed a gig on 52nd Street, New York's jazz alley. It was there that I covered her for the last time.

I arrived after eleven at night; and although Billie had been scheduled to start hours earlier, she had yet to appear onstage. In a way it didn't matter, for there were scarcely any customers. Word had spread that Billie's voice was shot and that, anyway, she had become unreliable and might not show—which seemed to be the case that night.

I still hoped to get a story and picture; so I snooped around the dressing rooms looking for Lady Day. I found her—alone, half dressed, and too far out of it to get herself together. At least, not without help.

I somehow managed to get her to the microphone. Then I wished I hadn't. I couldn't get myself to take notes. I couldn't get myself to take pictures.

Lady Day still had ten years left, and parts of them would be good. But that night on 52nd Street she seemed finished, and, in a sense, she was.

Billie at a concert performance.

Billie with her boxer, Mister.

Ella Fitzgerald

Ella with an "entranced" Dizzy Gillespie. The bassist is Ray Brown, to whom Ella was married. The head in the foreground belongs to Danish nobleman Timmie Rosenkrantz, mentioned earlier in the piece on The Lion.

Ella Fitzgerald is the perennial Queen of Jazz. Back in 1937 I made periodic pilgrimages to the Savoy Ballroom in Harlem to hear this singing phenomenon with the Cinderella background. (When only sixteen and an or-

phan, she won an amateur contest, joined the Chick Webb orchestra, and was adopted by Chick. At twenty, Ella recorded "A-tisket, A-tasket" and became world famous.)

Ella's boss and foster father, Chick Webb, was himself a phenomenon—a sickly hunchback who became one of the most dynamic drummers and leaders in jazz.

In 1939 Chick died and Ella took over the band for a short period, then became a single.

For several years she starred with Jazz at the Philharmonic, a touring concert group that did much to gain recognition for jazz as a form of serious music.

Ella's reign continued throughout the '40s. Her clear, swinging delivery lifted all but the most trivial songs into the realm of good music. Today, at the age of sixty, she is still Queen, filling concert halls at her personal appearances.

Ella, with an appropriate crown pendant.

Sarah "Sassy" Vaughan

Ella and Billie were two of the female voices that formed a divine triumvirate during the Golden Age of Jazz. The third: Sarah "Sassy" Vaughan.

Sassy was perhaps the most modern of the group; or, at least, she was the one who was the most warmly embraced by the boppers. Her innovative swoops and swirls formed an almost rococo ornamentation that appealed to the more progressive musicians.

Sometimes Sarah's daring convolutions left her tied inextricably in musical knots. But more often her adventures succeeded, adding great excitement to what was, to start with, an exceedingly rich and rhythmical voice.

The photos shown here were taken in 1946 when Sassy was still developing her remarkable style.

Ethel Waters had, by the '40s, become a popular actress who, when she sang at all, used very little jazz. Earlier, however, she was a successful blues singer who was accompanied by leading jazzmen and who inspired many young black performers.

Bertha "Chippie" Hill, who once sang with the King Oliver band and who had the likes of Louis Armstrong accompany her on blues records, dropped out of music in 1930, but was resurrected in the middle '40s, when there was a surge of interest in the roots of jazz.

Among white female vocalists, the first to be hailed by the jazz cognoscenti was Mildred Bailey (actually, she was part American Indian). Mildred, a big woman, sang with little-girl delicacy, but nonetheless managed to come across with a strong jazz feeling.

The most popular of the good band vocalists toward the end of the Golden Age was June Christy. Compared to Mildred Bailey, June's was a husky, driving, almost masculine delivery. It was a groove first developed by Anita O'Day, then adopted by many others. The photo impression shown here attempts to capture the emotional intensity June often achieved. For a more realistic picture, turn to the section on Stan Kenton, in the next chapter.

Another popular band singer was Doris Day. Doris, together with her longtime boss, Les Brown, was only marginally in the jazz field, but both she and Les *were* capable of delivering commendable music. At any rate, no need to shed tears for Doris. She went to Hollywood and was for several years the leading female box-office draw in the movie industry!

There were many fine singers during the Golden Age who, though they made recordings and kept busy at night clubs, were not big names. One representative of this group was Sylvia Syms, whose voice was compared at one time or another to Billie's, Sarah's, and Ella's! Another of the superior but relatively unknown singers was Dardanelle (just "Dardanelle"), a young Southerner with the proper manners of a Dixie dowager. Despite her reserve, Dardanelle led a swinging instrumental trio that featured her on vibraphone, piano, and vocals.

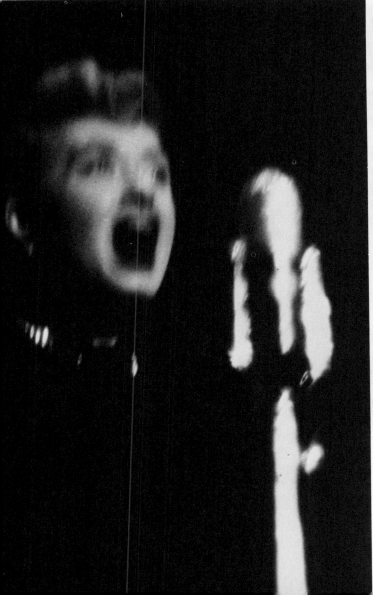

Mildred Bailey

June Christy

Dardanelle

Doris Day with Les Brown

Sylvia Syms

Most of the outstanding male jazz vocalists were instrumentalists who adapted their horn and keyboard phrasing to their singing. The pictures of many of the instrumentalist-singers appear elsewhere in this book; Louis Armstrong, who is pre-eminent among them, also appears *here,* as do several other outstanding examples of the genre: Jack Teagarden, Roy Eldridge, Nat Cole, and Joe Mooney.

Of all the instrumentalists who turned to singing, Nat Cole gained the greatest popular success. The fantastic reception given to such Cole records as "The Christmas Song" and "Nature Boy" led to his almost completely abandoning the piano. He concentrated instead on pop vocals, complete with lush string backgrounds; but his jazz-based style gave distinction to the most maudlin material.

Jack Teagarden

Louis Armstrong

Roy Eldridge

Nat "King" Cole

Joe Mooney

For me, the most underrated all-round jazz-man of the period was Joe Mooney. Joe, who was blind, could sing like a hip angel, write arrangements suitable for a heavenly combo, play the piano and organ divinely, and—most wonderful of all—squeeze jazz from an accordion, which is a miracle only slightly less wonderful than squeezing blood from a stone.

Joe paid his dues over the years by working for big bands in one or another of his several identities. Then in 1946 he formed a quartet, with himself handling the accordion and the vocals. The group was soon hailed by Mike Levin of *Down Beat* as "The most exciting musical unit in the U.S. today. . . . [Joe] is the best male vocalist on the scene. . . ." With

Mike's stupendous push, Joe quickly got choice club dates and a record contract. His quartet rocketed heavenward, where it belonged . . . only to fizzle and plunge back to earth, all in a matter of months. The quartet broke up, with one sideman retiring into a religious order.

Joe's problem was that his music was too quiet, too subtle. His suspenseful timing and sensitive inflections made his music jump like mad. But you had to *listen*. Carefully. And too few bothered.

Joe Mooney at accordion with Gaeton "Gate" Frega, left, at bass, and Andy Fitzgerald, right, clarinet. Missing: Jack Hotop, guitar.

Many of the best male vocalists were blues shouters, like Leadbelly and Big Joe Turner. "Mr. Five-by-Five," Jimmy Rushing, was another. Jimmy was the best known of the blues singers and certainly the best attached to a band. For many years he was a star of the Count Basie orchestra.

One of the few white men who unquestionably qualified as a singer of jazz was Mel Tormé. Mel started in music as a drummer, but soon devoted himself entirely to vocals. He retained, however, the well-grounded musicianship of a solid instrumentalist and was, therefore, much respected by the sidemen who accompanied him.

Mel was really different. He used unconventional phrasing that constantly surprised his audiences. With it went an unusual tone quality like that of a hushed foghorn. It earned him the appellation "The Velvet Fog." To take an appropriately foggy photo of him, I had him sing right above a dressing-room sink into which I had dropped a piece of dry ice.

Mel Tormé

Frank Sinatra

Frank Sinatra was snubbed by most of the serious jazz fans of the era, but they were wrong. The skinny kid who set the world on its ear when he sang with the Tommy Dorsey band had learned his craft thoroughly.

To his craftsmanship Frank added unerring good taste and the persistence of a perfectionist. At the recording date where the photos on these pages were taken, Frank rejected take after take. The session ran into an extra day before he was completely satisfied with his accompaniment, as well as with himself. The musicians with whom I checked assured me that he wasn't being peevishly difficult, nor was he taking advantage of Columbia Records, which was paying the bill; he simply knew exactly when a beat was mistimed or a section was out of balance.

Frank was probably the best singer the country produced during the Golden Age. He was not out to please jazz folk, so he felt free to pick songs that were outside the mainstream of hot music, and he made no attempt to convert his choices into jazz vehicles. Frank therefore didn't do what he would have had to do to be included with the jazz greats. But the man sang with a marvelous beat; his music swung. And, when he wanted to, he delivered what could truly qualify as hot music.

It should be noted that, musical qualities aside, Frank had a negative effect on jazz, for he, more than any other individual, brought about the decline of the big swing bands which had so stimulated all of jazz music. Economics had already doomed the big bands; their overhead had become too high. It was Frank who delivered the *coup de grâce* by making singers more important than bands. No longer merely vocalists who augmented the music made by orchestras, singers became the main attractions, with bands often reduced to the status of accompanists.

Babs Gonzales

Dave Lambert, at left, leading the Pastels, a group that sang with Stan Kenton.

Scat singing is the use by singers of non-sense syllables instead of words, with the syllables phrased as if coming from a jazz horn. Louis Armstrong was supposed to have invented scat when he forgot the lyrics of a song during a recording session.

During the '40s, scatting became widespread. Louis continued to lead the way; Ella, Leo Watson, and others followed. Some singers made scatting their specialty. The most intriguing of them was Babs Gonzales, who scatted in a bop groove. He was a composer, too. His biggest composition: "Oo-pa-pa-da."

Dave Lambert, a director of vocal groups and himself a singer, extended the use of voices-as-horns. He used actual words, as well as nonsense syllables, to produce the effects of a bop combo.

It's frequently difficult to decide which performer goes in what chapter of this book, and that's certainly true of Dave, Babs, June, Sarah, and many others, for they are not only singers but also part of the modern jazz world. Keep them in mind as you read the following chapter on modern jazz.

5. BOP!...
AND ALL THAT
MODERN JAZZ

No sooner had big-band swing established its sovereignty than dissidents revolted against it. As early as 1940 they condemned as sterile almost every cherished standard established during a half-century of jazz evolution. Why must there be the same old theme-with-variations format? they asked. Why must jazz be danceable? Why must it be entertaining? Melodious? Harmonious? Why must the drummer be required to maintain a solid, unswerving beat? Why stick to either two-four time or four-four time? Why not five-four? Or any other regular beat? Or *no* regular beat?

Nothing was sacred.

The revolutionaries formed two different groups, each with its own musical alternatives. The major group was, at least in its origins, entirely black; and its ideas, though radically new, were home-grown. If modern European "classical" concepts were at all worked into its sounds, this was done subconsciously.

The music of this group was called bebop, later abbreviated to *bop*. At first hearing, bop jarred the listener; he was unprepared for the onslaught. Bop was also devilishly difficult to play, with eccentric starts and stops; torrents of notes played at machine-gun tempos; and seemingly undisciplined solos relieved by rapid-fire unison choruses. This was jazz? Few of the established musicians thought so. Even fewer could play it, even when they tried.

The bop movement was a creation of the young—people in their teens and early twenties, like Kenny Clarke, Charlie Christian, Ken Kersey, Oscar Pettiford, and the three dominant personalities: Charlie Parker, Dizzy Gillespie, and Thelonious Monk. Bird was generally regarded as the intuitive genius and improviser of the group; Diz, the conscious thinker and showman; and Monk, the clearinghouse and refiner.

By the late 1940s, when big-band swing had declined, bop had matured and began to dominate the jazz scene. Commercially, and perhaps artistically, that scene was not nearly what it had once been. But the revolution did, in a sense, succeed.

The boppers' revolution was more than a musical upheaval. It was social, as well. James Lincoln Collier in his penetrating history *The Making of Jazz*, points out that the black men who created bop deliberately turned the old ways upside down in order to show their independence. Further, the modern black musician often acquired "cool" habits of language, dress, and behavior to help reinforce the impression that he was now an artist and no longer a mere entertainer. ". . . He eschewed anything that smacked of emotionalism. Not for him the grin and widespread arms of Armstrong; instead he coolly bowed to his audience at the end of a number and walked offstage."

The second revolutionary group—sometimes allied to but still quite different from the boppers—consisted mostly of whites. Its music, sometimes tagged "progressive jazz," deliberately incorporated the principles and devices of modern European "classical" music. The leaders included Stan Kenton, Dave Brubeck, Lennie Tristano, John Lewis (of the Modern Jazz Quartet), Woody Herman, Boyd Raeburn, and Claude Thornhill, though each was sufficiently different from the others so that they would probably have objected to my making them bedfellows.

Many critics felt that progressive jazz wasn't jazz at all, that it didn't swing . . . which was sometimes said about bop, too. Some modernists denied that their music didn't swing; others responded by asking: "Who says it has to?"

Whatever bop and progressive jazz may *not* have been, they definitely were the most vital forms of music to be found during the last years of the Golden Age.

(OPPOSITE) *Theolonious Monk at Minton's piano.*

Thelonious Sphere Monk

Some time in August 1947 it occurred to me that whereas Dizzy, Bird, and Thelonious were the most talked-about musicians of the day, only the first two were identities you could put your finger on. Dizzy was everywhere: the ubiquitous General of bop leading his various troops. Bird . . . well, when he wasn't in a hospital, he was playing club dates;

Mary Lou Williams'
"salon." At this particular
gathering, Mary Lou is
seated, center. From the
left: Dizzy Gillespie,
pianist-arranger Tadd
Dameron, pianist Hank
Jones. At far right:
trombonist Jack Teagarden.

Theolonious with Howard
McGhee, Roy Eldridge,
and Teddy Hill.

either way, you knew where *he* was. But what about Thelonious? No one I knew had seen him for nearly a year. Was he working somewhere? Sick? Was he even alive? Finding Thelonious became my special mission.

I found his mother's phone number and called. But she hadn't seen her boy for half a year. I located the last place he was known to have worked. But the manager said that ten months earlier Thelonious had gone out for a smoke during an intermission . . . and had yet to return.

There was more of same until I happened to mention my problem to Mary Lou Williams. Mary Lou, besides being a great piano player, was the focal point for musicians who wanted to keep up with what was happening. Jazz people were constantly dropping in at her apartment. It was a salon.

Mary Lou was just the person to provide a solution to my quest. "You want Thelonious? You'll *get* Thelonious." She rubbed her magic lantern and, sure enough, within a week Thelonious, very shy, showed up at my Rockefeller Center office.

Unfortunately, the setting unnerved Monk, and my interview floundered. So we shifted, via taxi, to Minton's Playhouse, an undistinguished-looking night club in Harlem. It was at Minton's that bop had actually been incubated some six or seven years earlier. (Probably never before in history had a complete art movement been created in a single room.)

Once Thelonious felt relaxed, he proved to be articulate and informative. He told me that the club had been founded by Henry Minton, the first black delegate to Local 802 of the musicians' union, and that Teddy Hill, a former swing-band leader, took over the management of the club in 1940. Though Teddy's own tastes were conservative, he encouraged the most iconoclastic musicians to drop in and jam, even providing them with free food on Mondays (when musicians with jobs had the night off). Teddy figured that if the hippest musicians made Minton's their hangout, paying customers would come to listen. He was right, so he kept the place congenial to musicians with experimental proclivities. Before long, even the top white jazzmen showed up to find out what was new, and to join in the jam sessions. Supposedly, some of the trickiest and most radical inventions in bop were deliberately developed by Minton's black regulars just to frustrate the visiting big-name whites and keep them, with their big reputations, from dominating the Monday-night sessions.

In any case, Minton's prospered and the new music burgeoned. Suddenly Teddy Hill found himself the guardian angel of bop.

At Minton's, Thelonious had acted as a kind of house pianist and resident composer. He was also the respected guru to whom visiting musicians came with their latest ideas, to have them appraised and refined. Pianos are well suited for working on musical problems, so it was largely around Monk and his piano that the new music developed. I photographed Thelonious playing on the very instrument where it had all happened.

During my conversation with Thelonious, trumpeter Howard McGhee dropped around, then trumpeter Roy Eldridge and manager Teddy Hill. Howard got Monk to dream up some horn passages and then persuaded him to write them down on score sheets. That's one of the ways musicians made use of Monk's overflowing creative talents.

Teddy Hill pulled me aside and spoke about Thelonious. "He's the guy who deserves the most credit for creating bop. I know. I was there."

I never did find out where Monk had been through the previous months, but Teddy indirectly explained Thelonious' mysterious ways. "He's completely absorbed in thinking about music. Maybe he's on the way to meet you. An idea comes to him. He begins to work on it. Mop! Days go by and he's still at it. He's forgotten all about you and everything else but that idea."

Soon after the session at Minton's, I placed illustrated articles on Monk in *Down Beat*, the *Record Changer*, and the *Saturday Review*. As a result of the publicity, Thelonious was offered several gigs. He was once again back on the music scene, and there he stayed—more or less. The one time I went to see Monk at work, he didn't quite recognize me. It didn't matter. I had accomplished what I had set out to do. I had found Thelonious Sphere Monk.

Charlie Parker with bassist Tommy Potter.

Charles "Yardbird" Parker

Bird was widely acknowledged to be the supreme jazz genius of his time. He was also widely acknowledged to be the most self-destructive. Drugs. Alcohol. You name it. But somehow his musical talents prevailed over his worst excesses. When he was blowing, Bird could effortlessly produce chorus after chorus of wondrous improvisations. He could turn standard tunes into amazing melodies no one had ever heard before.

The accompanying photos of Bird were taken soon after he returned East from a long stay in Camarillo, a California hospital where he had recovered from a major breakdown. Despite a strange look in his eyes, he never was healthier or more relaxed. But, in time, he again pushed the self-destruct button. Bird slowly fell apart and died at age thirty-five. Significantly, the attending physician took him to be a man in his mid-fifties.

Bird with his ardent disciple, trumpeter Robert "Red" Rodney. In the mirror: Dizzy Gillespie.

Dizzy's battle regalia. (The now famous uptilted horn came later.)

John Birks "Dizzy" Gillespie

You'd think from his nickname and his on-stage antics that Dizzy Gillespie was the wildest of the many wild bop musicians. Not so. He was, on the contrary, practical-minded, singularly dependable, and intelligent.

Not that he didn't deserve the name *Dizzy*. But that went back to his exuberant younger days. There was the much repeated story involving, of all things, a spitball that *someone* threw while the Cab Calloway band was performing in a theater. In the ensuing argument Diz nicked Cab with a knife.

Or there were the frantic times when an even younger Gillespie worked for Teddy Hill. Teddy once gave me some details: "Right off, at his first rehearsal, he began to play in an overcoat, hat, and gloves. For a while, everyone was set against this maniac. Me, too. I gave him the name 'Dizzy.'

"When I took my band to Europe, some of the guys threatened not to go if the crazy one went, too. But by then I realized that, with all his eccentricities and practical jokes, he was the most stable of us all. Sure enough, he turned out to be the one with the cleanest habits and the best business sense. He saved so much money in Europe that he encouraged the others to borrow from him, just so he'd have an income in case things got rough back in the States: Diz crazy? Diz was crazy like a fox."

It was almost a sacred obligation for modern musicians to be cool. But Diz couldn't contain his antic spirits. He hammed up his performances as much as did Armstrong before him. And whereas some modern-jazz theologians advocated austere banker's-gray suits, Diz made a uniform out of a beret, heavy-rimmed glasses, and a Vandyke beard. Hundreds of other boppers emulated him.

Diz's original contributions went beyond things sartorial. He showed that bop, which started as music for small combos, would work successfully with big bands. He then showed that there was a place in jazz orchestras for Afro-Cuban rhythms. And, above all, he showed that a trumpet could be used in remarkable new ways.

Diz's playing was incredible: gushes of extremely rapid notes, each cleanly articulated, and the whole of it making good jazz sense instead of being a mere display of virtuosity. And leave it to Diz to do it in his own peculiar way. A trumpet player's lips and tongue and cheeks—his embouchure—is supposed to be held in, tightly. But Dizzy puffed his cheeks like balloons. And that neck! On the strong notes, it bulged until it actually looked as if it would burst. Everything was wrong with his playing, except the results.

It was inevitable that Diz, the colorful yet dependable genius, would assume the leadership of the bop movement. This he did with confidence and flair. And when bop took over 52nd Street toward the end of the '40s, Diz just naturally became King of The Street.

Diz at full blast: cheeks ballooning, neck bulging.

Dizzy Gillespie,
King of "The Street."

Stan Kenton

Stan Kenton was the most prominent of those modern jazzmen whose music was consciously influenced by "classical" forms. Stan had at least one other distinction: he was the most controversial of the modern music makers.

Those who couldn't stand his orchestra found it pretentious, devoid of swing, and just plain awful. Yet such denigrations could, at worst, characterize only his more formal concert pieces. Most of his music over the years *did* swing—enough so that his orchestra was voted best swing band of the year in the *Down Beat* polls of 1947, 1950, 1951, 1952, 1953, and 1954!

It is a fact that his music, which he called "progressive jazz," often favored tightly written scores over improvisation; mixed tempos over strict time; and still other characteristics associated more with European music than with American jazz. In particular, he was not beholden to the big beat. "It's not the rhythm that counts," he would say, "It's the personalized warmth of the sound." To paraphrase Duke: "It don't mean a thing if it ain't got that warmth." But *was* his music warm? His numerous detractors protested that it was absolutely cold!

Warm or cold, it was loud. Stan's screaming horns presaged the high decibels of the rock age, but his stalwarts did it without electronic amplification. Just old-fashioned lung power. When Stan raised his long arms to call for "more," the men in the brass section blew until their faces reddened, their eyes bulged, and incipient hernias popped.

I once spent nearly a week with Stan and his orchestra doing one-nighters. One-nighters were—and probably still are—a remunerative but baneful part of every "name" orchestra's existence. It meant traveling hundreds of miles a day, day after day for weeks, playing a dance here on one night, a concert there on

the next night, and so on, the fees and distances depending on the popularity of the band and the skills of the band's booking agent.

One-nighters could turn into a rigorous, wearisome regimen for the musicians of any orchestra. It was even tougher for the members of the Kenton band, for Stan was a perfectionist driven by two inextricably connected forces: a desire for personal success and a crusade for progressive jazz.

Typically, the band would play, say, a concert, ending at eleven P.M. Stan would give the group a short break, but get it back for a strenuous rehearsal lasting an hour or so. Only then were the musicians released. Generally, they'd go—where else?—to a local music spot for a late snack and to hear what the local cats were blowing.

Then to their hotel. Late to bed. Late to rise. After breakfast, musicians and wives into bus. Instruments into truck. Next town, maybe 150 miles away. Where's Stan? Up early. Raced ahead in own car, like the wind (me along, a little scared). Interview with reporter. Visit to college music department. Session with one, two local disc-jockeys. Stan very bright. Very persuasive. By now, gang has arrived. Check in at hotel. Time and weather permitting, a quick game of intra-band baseball. But not for Stan. He's phoning ahead. Interviews to set for tomorrow, 200 miles away. Now it's concert time. Or dance time. Then it starts all over again.

Some days are a little different. Like that night we went to a club and got talking to a trio of college students, a little drunk, who made it clear they didn't like Kenton's music. I left the club a minute after the rest. Seeing me leave alone and thinking I was part of the band, the trio jumped me. I yelled. Eddie Safranski, an average-sized fellow made husky by wrestling a bass, rushed in like a squad of marines. Very gutsy. End of students.

A week to remember.

Stan Kenton and Marion "Buddy" Childers photographed through a fractured mirror to suggest the shattering effect of the Kenton band's loud, dissonant brass.

The band on a concert date, with wives—and even a child—in the wings.

Laurindo Almeida was a "classical" concert artist, as well as the Kenton guitarist. Stan, along with Dizzy Gillespie, was one of the first to blend Latin rhythms with jazz.

Shelly Manne in two moods.

*Kai Winding, one of the
band's super-musicians.*

*June Christy. Compare
this photo with the
impressionistic shot in the
chapter on vocalists.*

*Eddie Safranski on a dance date, where the audience
could crowd up close to the band.*

Pete Rugolo, the band's chief arranger.

Sometimes the camera caught a fleeting drama enacted by the "dancers."

A midnight rehearsal backstage.

Passing time in the bus, on the way to the next one-nighter.

Stan at one of the many daily interviews.

Recreation time. Rugolo at bat.

Stan reviewing the next day's plans with Bob Gioga, the band's road manager and baritone sax.

The two groups of modernists—the boppers and progressives—were not always easily differentiated. Some of their members straddled both camps. Others kept one foot planted in earlier forms of jazz. The next few pages display photos of some of those musicians with whom I came in contact who were identified with modern jazz, whatever their specific cubicle might have been.

Max Roach was the greatest of the bop drummers.

Theodore "Fats" Navarro, trumpet, died at 26—a tragic genius in the Charlie Parker mold. Tadley "Tadd" Dameron, center, was probably bopland's favorite arranger. The tenor is Charles Rouse; the alto, Ernie Henry.

Allen Eager was closely associated with Tadd and Fats, as well as with several swing bands.

Milton "Bags" Jackson. His vibraharp was the dominant voice of the Modern Jazz Quartet. The bassist in this photo is Ray Brown.

John Lewis, shown here at the piano, began his career in bop, arranging and playing for the big band of Dizzy Gillespie. He then became famous as the creator of the Modern Jazz Quartet, the ultra-cool combo that was steeped in classical forms. Behind John is baritone sax Cecil Payne; behind Cecil, Miles Davis. (Note the Ellington portrait painted on Diz's tie.)

(ABOVE LEFT) *Bill De Arango was a modern guitarist with outstanding technical skills. Terry Gibbs was, along with Bags, the top young vibes artist of the era.*

(ABOVE RIGHT) *Chuck Wayne was the star guitarist of many groups, including the George Shearing quintet.*

(RIGHT) *Barbara Carroll, pianist, was probably the first female bop musician. For a while she led a trio that featured Chuck Wayne.*

Billy Taylor, a remarkably versatile jazz figure, played with top swing, Latin, and bop combos, eventually developing a uniquely smooth bop style. He later tripled as a disc-jockey and as a lecturer on the history of jazz.

Eli "Lucky" Thompson
continually alternated
between bop and
conventional jazz grooves.
The bassist is Al
McKibbon, one of the best
in the business.

Oscar Pettiford was one of
the bop pioneers at
Minton's. He and Diz
jointly led the first bop
band to play 52nd Street
(1943).

Boniface "Buddy" De Franco was one of the few modernists on the clarinet, an instrument that greatly declined in popularity by the late '40s.   Here he's working on the portable piano he carried on trips.

Billy "Mr. B" Eckstine, best known as a singer, led an orchestra
that, at various times, included Charlie Parker, Sarah Vaughan,
Dizzy Gillespie, Fats Navarro, Miles Davis, Art Blakey, Tadd
Dameron, Lucky Thompson, and Dexter Gordon.

Georgie Auld moved progressively from swing to modern music. Here he's leading a combo that featured several illustrious boppers. At left is Serge Chaloff, on baritone; on trumpet, Red Rodney; on drums, Norman "Tiny" Kahn.

Joseph "Flip" Phillips, known for his crowd-rousing tenor, is shown fronting an all-star combo consisting of Bill Harris, trombone, a giant at his instrument; Denzil Best, drums, long a key man with the Shearing quintet; Billy Bauer, guitar, a frequent poll winner; Greig "Chubby" Jackson, bass, the popular dynamo of many rhythm sections; and Lennie Tristano, piano, who, though blind, was one of the most distinctive modern theorists and the leader of a musically radical cult.

Charlie Ventura made his name as tenor sax with Gene Krupa, then led a number of exciting combos. He shared the leadership of one group with trombonist Bill Harris.

The unusual orchestra of Claude Thornhill included French horns and other exotic instruments. Many of the musicians were prominent jazzmen. Danny Polo is at the rear, second from left; Lee Konitz, one of Tristano's leading disciples, third from left. Other Thornhill jazzmen were Gerry Mulligan and Gil Evans, neither one shown here.

Here, except for Pete Rugolo, are all the top arrangers for the big, modern, white orchestras: (from the top) Eddie Sauter, Ed Finckel, George Handy, Johnny Richards, Neal Hefti, Ralph Burns.

Boyd Raeburn led the farthest-out big band of the period. At one time or another, his sidemen included musicians like Dizzy Gillespie and Buddy De Franco. His arrangers, Ed Finckel, George Handy, and Johnny Richards, were extraordinary.

Woody Herman had several "Herds" and used several separate styles. During one period he went heavily into progressive, European-oriented music. Igor Stravinsky wrote "Ebony Concerto" for him. Shown here at a rehearsal are Walter Hendl of the National Symphony Orchestra, who conducted the premiere of the concerto; Tony Aless, piano; Billy Bauer, guitar; Chubby Jackson, bass; Don Lamond, drums; Woody Herman, clarinet; Flip Phillips, tenor.

Miles Davis with Howard McGhee

Miles Davis

What better way to conclude this book than with Miles Davis? He was, after all, the last star of the Golden Age of Jazz, as well as the brightest star of eras that followed.

Let's go back to a day in 1947 at Nola's rehearsal studio, where I chanced upon Howard McGhee, a top bop trumpet. Howard was working with other musicians on some new charts. I happened to have my camera and took several shots, in one of which I included a young onlooker—a handsome fellow with intense, piercing eyes. I had no idea who he was and, since I didn't use the picture, forgot about him . . . until thirty-two years later, when, while going through my picture files, I recognized the face. He was the person who

became what critic Jim Collier recently described as "perhaps the most important trend-setter in the history of Jazz." The piercing eyes belonged, of course, to Miles Davis, age twenty.

By the time Miles was twenty-one, it was impossible *not* to recognize him. He had become the most sought-after of modern trumpet players. When Coleman Hawkins, an elder statesman of jazz, probed the new sounds, he hired young Miles as his trumpet man. When Charlie Parker could no longer get Diz to play with him, he got Miles. Later, when Diz built his big orchestra, he chose Miles to back him up. And when Gerry Mulligan, Gil Evans, and other Thornhill alumni were looking for

Miles Davis with Coleman Hawkins

an inspired trumpet to lead their new group in a recording that would launch "cool jazz," they, too, turned to Miles.

Miles' most acclaimed inventions were to come in a period not covered by this book. But his talent and aggressive individuality were apparent long before the end of the '40s. He had by then established himself as the coolest of the cool cats, not only in his playing but in his behavior: on the job, Miles displayed an unmistakable "drop dead" attitude. He'd blow his horn. Period. No singing. No dance steps. No jokes. No flamboyant clothes. No flashing teeth. He kept real cool, man. But, obviously, there was a hot flame burning behind those piercing eyes.

Miles Davis with Charlie Parker

INDEX

[Numbers printed in italic type refer to illustrations.]

ABOUT THE AUTHOR

William P. Gottlieb's first contact with jazz came in 1936 while writing a monthly record page for the Lehigh University *Review*. He then went to work for *The Washington Post*, producing, among other things, a weekly music column—one of the first regular newspaper features devoted primarily to jazz. At the same time, he performed as a disc jockey on Washington's NBC outlet, WRC, and on an independent station, WINX.

After the war, he became a writer for the music magazine *Down Beat*, and wrote about jazz not only for the *Beat* but for the *Record Changer*, the *Saturday Review*, and *Colliers*.

Throughout the Golden Age of Jazz, Bill Gottlieb was the only reporter who was taking pictures and getting stories at the same time. This book presents the best of the remarkable photographs he took during those years.